We Read: A to Z

Donald Crews

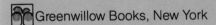 Greenwillow Books, New York

Library of Congress Cataloging in Publication Data

Crews, Donald. We read.

Summary: Each letter of the alphabet introduces a concept that is also represented by an illustration.   1. English language—Alphabet—Juvenile literature.   2. Vocabulary—Juvenile literature.   [1. Alphabet]   I. Title.
PE1155.C73   1984   [E]   83-25453
ISBN 0-688-03843-3   ISBN 0-688-03844-1 (lib. bdg.)

Particularly for Ann, Nina, Amy,
Donna, Janine, Malcolm, Michael, and Zönke

From the
alphabet, with
just twenty-six
letters, A to Z,
all words
are made.

Aa, almost: nearly all red

1

Bb, bottom: where the green is

2

Cc, corner: where the yellow is

3

Dd, double: always two, always the same

4

Ee, equal:
as many black
as yellow

5

Ff, few:
not many
squares

6

Gg, grow: things get bigger

7

Hh, horizontal: from side to side

8

li, inside:
where the
black is

9

Jj, jagged: sharp points

10

Kk, kind: same shape, different color

11

LI, left:
the half
where the
blue is

12

Mm, middle: the center from any direction

13

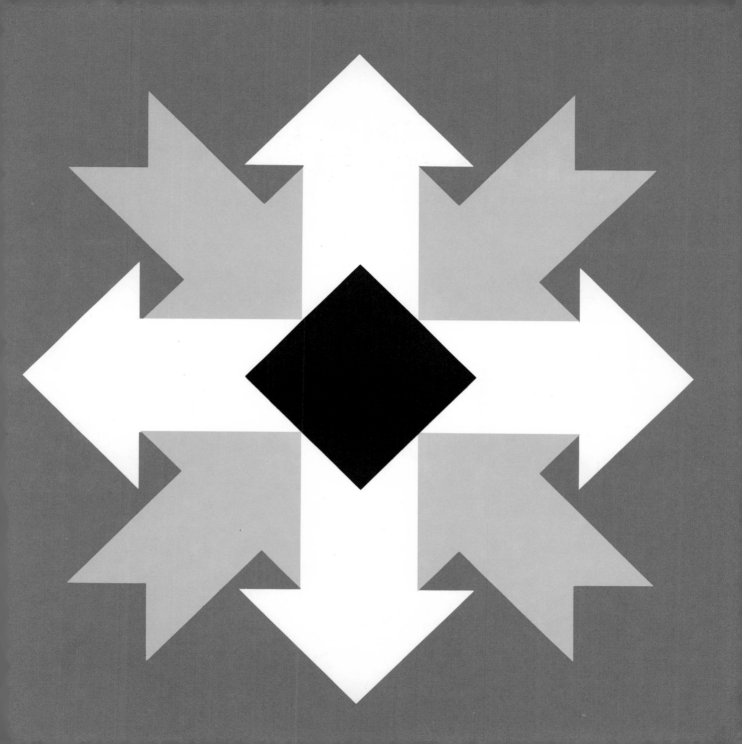

Nn, nothing:

14

Oo, over: where the black is

15

Pp, parts: pieces separated

16

Qq, quarters:
four equal parts

17

Rr, right:
the half
where the
blue is

18

Ss, size:
one large,
one small

19

Tt, top: where the blue is

20

Uu, under: where the black is

21

Vv, vertical: up and down

22

Ww, whole:
in one piece

23

Xx, extra: one square left over

24

Yy, only: just one

25

Zz, zigzag: looks as it sounds

26